Most churches and church leaders "tellers" as we work with groups ar. has the potential of truly transforming the individual and the church through internal creative change. We invited Tim and Mike to train our Life Group volunteer coaches to maximize their effectiveness. Through asking the right questions, our newly trained coaches are taking our Life Group ministry to a brand new level.

Dr. Brad Kalajainen
Lead Pastor, Cornerstone Church
Caledonia, MI

The concepts in *Coaching Based Ministry* will transform the methods used in any helping service. No longer a teacher who only tells, I now ask questions, lead students to possibilities, and am thrilled at their positive response. Want to strengthen a relationship or see better results at work? This guide will identify the steps you can take to lead others to empowerment.

Ginger Sisson
Software Trainer, Follett Software Co.
Grand Rapids, MI

Tim and Mike have written a great introduction to doing ministry with a Christ-centered, peer coaching model. If you desire to help others change and become what God has designed them to be, then you can use this resource. The Christ-centered explanations will help ministry leaders use a coaching lens to see how Jesus engaged in conversations and empowered people. A great resource for anyone working to facilitate growth and change in the lives of others.

David R. Beach, M.A.
Co-author, *The Essential Bible Companion to the Psalms*

Coaching Based Ministry is a great tool to help anyone learn the benefits and techniques of life coaching. The wisdom found here allows me to challenge students to focus on their present situations and set realistic goals to better their life using Godly principles. Too many people get discouraged by trying to live up to the advice of others instead of figuring out their desired goals and steps on their own. With intentional questions and accountability, this book trains anyone to be effective in reaching out to people and making significant change.

Jodie Gazan
Campus Life Ministry Director
Grand Rapids, MI

The coaching approach to ministry in this book takes the burden off the coach and encourages the person being coached to turn to God. This book provides a blueprint that will revolutionize your ministry. Create a culture of coaching with the empowering principles of *Coaching Based Ministry*. You and those you minister to will never be the same.

Dr. Mark Vander Meer
Executive Director
Community Recovery International

COACHING BASED
MINISTRY

COACHING BASED
MINISTRY

Transforming Ministry
Through **Empowerment Coaching**

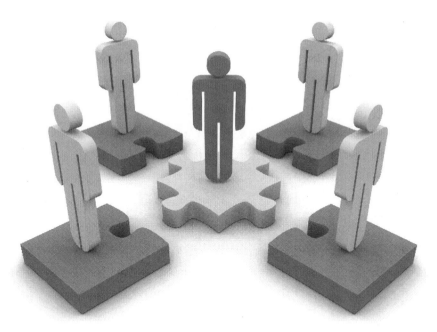

MIKE McGERVEY AND TIM COSBY

credo
house publishers

Coaching Based Ministry ™

Published in the United States by Credo House Publishers,a division of
Credo Communications, LLC, Grand Rapids, Michigan.
www.credohousepublishers.com

Published in partnership with Empowerment Coaching Network LLC.

Empowerment Coaching Network's mission is to bring Christ-centered,
peer coaching to the church. To respond to the message of this book, for more
information about the ministry, and for details on how to order additional copies
of *Coaching Based Ministry*, please contact us at:
Empowerment Coaching Network LLC
2341 Lakehurst St., N.E.
Grand Rapids, MI 49525
Email: timlifecoach@gmail.com
www.empowermentcoachingnetwork.com

ISBN: 978-1-935391-62-3

Cover design by Frank Gutbrod
Interior design and composition by Frank Gutbrod

Printed in the United States of America
First Edition

CONTENTS

WHY COACHING?

INTRODUCTION

Let's be clear. We believe that *coaching* is the single most effective process for guiding spiritual transformation, personal growth, and leader development. We are also convinced that as churches and faith-based organizations discover the power and possibilities of coaching, there will be a growing effort to rebuild ministries and develop leaders around what we call the *Coaching-Based Ministry*™ model.

The Merriam-Webster online dictionary defines *ministry* as "the office, duties, or functions of a minister." That tells us nothing about the process and practice of ministry. We much prefer a definition that J. R. Briggs (jrbriggs.com) learned in one of his early seminary classes . . .

"Meeting people where they are and taking them to where God wants them to be."

That definition tells us three very important truths about ministry.

- Ministry begins where people are, not where we think they should be.

- Ministry is focused on where God wants them to be, not on where we think they should be.
- The key phrase is "taking them." That begs the question: what is the most effective approach for "taking them" from where they are to where God wants them to be?

Traditional models of spiritual transformation and leader development depend on the ability of experts to impart their knowledge, experience, and advice to others. But what we have discovered is that receiving information and advice alone does not lead to transformation and growth. This happens only when a person becomes internally motivated to change.

Coaching empowers people to change without telling them what to do. To be empowered means to take ownership of and responsibility for shaping your own future. This is based on the principle that the people you coach will understand, value, and apply for themselves what you help them to discover, not what you tell them.

As Ephesians 2:10 reminds us, *"we are God's handiwork, created in Christ Jesus to do good works, which God prepared in advance for us to do."* The *Coaching-Based Ministry Model* says this: God is at work in my life, and God is at work in your life. The best way I can help you discover the good works that God has prepared in advance for you to do is by coaching.

We are both professional coaches with many stories to tell about the impact coaching has had both on us and on the people we coach. We are also cofounders of *The Empowerment Coaching Network* , with the mission of bringing Christ-centered peer coaching to the church. We meet weekly with church and faith-based organization leaders to share our vision for *Coaching-Based Ministry*, and each month we equip people to coach through our sixteen-hour *Empowerment Coaching Training* program.

From these experiences we have learned that helping people let go of traditional thinking about ministry and grasp the significance of a coaching-based approach presents a real challenge. That's what led us to write this book.

This book is built around helping you find answers to three key questions.

- Why coaching?
- What is it like to be coached?
- What does it take to become an effective coach?

It is our hope and prayer that you will find meaningful answers to those questions and will then join us in bringing *Coaching-Based Ministry*™ to the churches and faith-based organizations in your area.

Mike McGervey & Tim Cosby

2

I DON'T GET WHAT YOU DO

Sharen, a Life Coach and one of our *Empowerment Coaching Training* graduates, shared the following story with us:

My nine-year old grandson was attending day camp near our home while his parents were on vacation. On his last morning with us, he bounded onto our bed and began chattering about things on his mind. At one point he exclaimed, "Gram, I SO don't get what you do as a life coach!" I asked, "Well, how about if I coach you so you can see what it's like?" He was immediately up for the challenge. Like any good life coach, I began by asking him to share some of his life dreams. His first response was, "I don't know what I dream of doing. What do you mean?" "Well, that's just what many of my clients say. Let's talk some more about your dreams."

Here's how the initial conversation went between Coach Gram and Client Grandson . . .

Me: Is there anything you long to do or accomplish? What would that look like?

Him: OH! I'd like to collect a thousand Pokémon cards! You mean like that?

Me: Yes, like that. How might you go about building your collection? How could we close the gap of where you are right now, having no cards, and where you want to be, having one thousand cards?

Him: Well, I could collect a few at a time.

Me: How many do you think you could collect in a week's time?
Him: Probably about ten.

Me: Great. So by the next time we meet, you'll have purchased ten new Pokémon cards?

Him: (Gaining enthusiasm) Yes, by next week!

Fast forward to our meeting the following week . . .

Me: How'd it go with your action step of collecting ten new cards?

Him: Not so good (a disappointed frown on his face).

Me: How come?

Him: Well, I spent my money on ice cream instead!

Me: Oh! Got ya. So, what could you do to catch up and still get your cards for this week?

Him: I'd have to not buy ice cream.

Me: Right! What else?

Him: I could do a job for Mom and Dad for more money.

Me: So, I hear you saying you will not buy any ice cream next week, and you will do some work for extra money. Your goal for next week is twenty cards, ten from last week plus ten for next week. Right?

Him: Yes, that's it.

Fast forward again to our third meeting . . .

Me: How'd it go with your goal of getting twenty Pokémon cards this past week?

Him: GREAT! I'm all caught up on my action steps . . . twenty cards, and ready for next week.

Me: That's super; I'm really proud of you! I'll be here to keep cheering you on to your goal of a thousand Pokémon cards.

Him: Now I get it! I get what you do, Gram!

Think for a moment about what enabled Sharen's nine-year old grandson to make the mental paradigm shift from "I don't understand what you do" to "Now I get it." She didn't haul out her PowerPoint and flip chart and give him a lecture about coaching. She coached him, and through that experience he discovered for himself what she does.

Tucked away in the back of his mind was his dream of collecting one thousand Pokémon cards. For a nine-year old, that was one big bodacious goal. You can bet he had been thinking about it for some time. Consider what happened when Sharen began coaching him.

- He quickly went from thinking about it to doing something about it.
- He clearly answered the question "What specifically do you want to accomplish?"
- He defined the weekly action steps he wanted to accomplish.
- He identified the obstacles blocking his progress and decided what he could do to break through and move ahead.
- He learned an important lesson about making wise choices.
- From his coach he received praise, encouragement, and the promise to keep cheering him on until he achieved his goal.

Not once did Sharen tell her grandson what he should do. Instead, she asked questions that enabled him to define and take responsibility for pursuing his dream. He was empowered. Quite an experience for a nine-year old, wouldn't you say? Why coaching? Ask Sharen's grandson.

Our experience tells us that everyone is driven by goals, either their own or someone else's. Too many of us have spent too much of our lives pursuing the goals and expectations others have set for us. One of the great benefits of being coached is that the "I sure would like to . . . " and "If only I could . . . " thoughts rolling around in the back of our minds are brought to the surface and transformed into achievable goals. We can now go from being *pushed* by the goals and expectations of others to being *pulled* toward achieving goals that are meaningful and important to us. And right there beside us is our coach, helping us to define those goals, explore options, make wise choices, overcome obstacles, achieve weekly action steps, and celebrate our achievements.

Why coaching? Because there is no better way to help someone transform their dreams into reality.

As we stated in the Introduction, we believe that coaching is the single most effective process for guiding spiritual transformation, personal growth, and leader development. Imagine that in your church, or in the faith-based organizations where you work or volunteer, a growing number of people are being equipped to coach anyone of any age who comes to them for any type of help. As you consider what Sharen's nine-year old grandson experienced, what do you think the impact of Coaching-Based Ministry™ could be?

Our dream is that as you continue reading this book you too will be able to say with clarity, "Now I get it!"

The Coach asks . . .

- What "I sure would like to . . . " and "If only I could . . . " thoughts do you have tucked away in the back of your mind?

- What would it mean for you to go from being *pushed* by the goals and expectations of others to being *pulled* by your own passions, interests, and goals?

- Reflecting on what Sharen's nine-year old grandson experienced, how might you benefit from being coached in one of those "I sure would like to . . . " areas?

- Thinking about the ministries in your church, what would the potential impact be if the people who lead and do ministry were equipped to coach anyone who came to them for help?

▶ Read on.

3

JESUS COACHED

An important coaching principle is to refrain from assuming anything about the person you are coaching. There are key aspects of their past you do not know, and you certainly don't know where God wants them to be. This was not the case with Jesus, as evidenced by His encounter with the Samaritan women at the well. After talking with Jesus, she went back to the town and said to the people there, *"Come, see a man who told me everything I ever did"* (John 4:29).

Jesus was not a coach in the sense that we are, but Jesus coached. In spite of being able to give perfect advice, He frequently chose to create teachable moments by asking questions. He did so not to gain knowledge about these persons but to empower them to gain insights into themselves. More often than not, an encounter with Jesus became a moment of self-discovery. Note these two examples.

- *"He asked his disciples, 'Who do people say the Son of Man is?' They replied, 'Some say John the Baptist; others say Elijah; and still others, Jeremiah or one of the prophets.' 'But what about you?' he asked. 'Who do you say I am?'"*—Matthew 16:13–15

- *"If you love those who love you, what credit is that to you? . . . And if you do good to those who are good to you, what credit is that to you? . . . And if you lend to those from whom you expect repayment, what credit is that to you?"* —Luke 6:32–34

This *coach approach* evolves out of asking open-ended questions to probe, expand, and focus the thinking of the person you are coaching. Already in Genesis 3 we find God asking Adam and Eve three probing questions: Where are you? Who told you that you were naked? Have you eaten from the tree I commanded you not to eat from?

God already knew the answers, but He also knew that for Adam and Eve to grow in their understanding of their relationship with Him they needed to think about and take responsibility for their choices. God was challenging them to follow Him from the heart, and heart transformation requires an internal motivation to change, not just responding to external advice and expectations. God asked questions, listened to their responses, guided them toward a solution, and showed them the way out of the mess they had made. He made atonement for their sin by killing an animal and provided clothing to cover their nakedness.

The *coach approach* involves using open-ended questions to get people to stop in their tracks and think about what they are doing and where they are headed. As you journey through the Old Testament, you often find God using questions for this "stop and think" purpose. Here are a few examples.

- **Moses**—when he was refusing God's job offer for him to lead Israel out of Egyptian bondage. *"Then the LORD's anger burned against Moses and he said, 'What about your brother, Aaron the Levite? I know he can speak well.'"* —Exodus 4:14

- **Joshua**—when he thought the Israelites would be conquered by the Amorites. *"The LORD said to Joshua, 'Stand up! What are you doing down on your face?'"* — Joshua 7:10
- **Samuel**—when he continued to mourn over Saul. *"The LORD said to Samuel, 'How long will you mourn for Saul, since I have rejected him as king over Israel?'"* —1 Samuel 16:1
- **Isaiah**—when he was deciding whether to answer God's call to prophesy to his own people. *"Then I heard the voice of the Lord saying, 'Whom shall I send? And who will go for us?' And I said, 'Here am I. Send me!'"* —Isaiah 6:8
- **Jeremiah**—when he was deciding whether to answer God's call to prophesy to the nations. *"The word of the LORD came to me: 'What do you see, Jeremiah?' 'I see the branch of an almond tree,' I replied."* —Jeremiah 1:11

This pattern is repeated throughout the Old Testament, but it isn't until we encounter the life of Jesus that we truly begin to see the power of the coaching model being used to motivate and develop others, including leaders. It didn't seem to matter with whom Jesus was conversing; He always had a question for them. Matthew records 65 questions; Mark, 45; Luke, 73; and John, 45. Each of the questions Jesus asked challenged the person to stop and think about something that had life-changing implications. It wasn't the verbal response given but the change in life direction that mattered. For example, imagine He is asking you each of the following questions.

- *You of little faith, why are you so afraid?* Matthew 8:26
- *Do you believe that I am able to do this?* Matthew 9:28
- *How many loaves do you have?* Matthew 15:34
- *Who do you say I am?* Matthew 16:15

- *What do you want me to do for you?* Matthew 20:32
- *Do you still not understand?* Mark 8:21
- *What good is it for someone to gain the whole world, yet forfeit their soul? Or what can anyone give in exchange for their soul?* Mark 8:36–37
- *Why are you trying to trap me?* Mark 12:15
- *If you love those who love you, what credit is that to you?* Luke 6:32
- *Why do you look at the speck of sawdust in your brother's eye and pay no attention to the plank in your own eye?* Luke 6:41
- *If you then, though you are evil, know how to give good gifts to your children, how much more will your Father in heaven give the Holy Spirit to those who ask him!* Luke 11:13
- *Who of you by worrying can add a single hour to your life?* Luke 12:25
- *Why are you troubled, and why do doubts rise in your minds?* Luke 24:38
- *Do you have anything here to eat?* Luke 24:41
- *Do you want to get well?* John 5:6
- *Where shall we buy bread for these people to eat?* John 6:5
- *Simon son of John, do you love me?* John 21:16
- *Saul, Saul, why do you persecute me?* Acts 9:4

There are a number of stories in Scripture where Jesus uses the *coach approach* to effect spiritual transformation. Here are two.

1. The first is found in Luke 24. It serves as a powerful example of how Jesus helps people to change without telling them what to do.

   After the crucifixion and resurrection, two disciples were walking from Jerusalem to their home in Emmaus.

Notice how Jesus coaches these two followers back into joy and mission. He joins them on the road and asks a simple question: *What are you discussing together as you walk along?* We read that they *"stood still, their faces downcast."* With that simple probing question, Jesus was asking, "Do you hear what you're saying? Do you know how your perception of reality has affected your speech?" This is a great coaching question because when our perspective is skewed or based on something that isn't true, it affects everything. Those disciples thought that the "Hope of Israel" was dead . . . and that their hopes had died with Him.

Jesus listened to them long enough to discover that the recent events in Jerusalem had severely shaken their beliefs. Then he asked another question: *"Did not the Messiah have to suffer these things and then enter his glory?"* They knew about the suffering Messiah prophesied by Isaiah, but they hadn't yet connected the dots to Jesus. Jesus helped them to realign their beliefs with reality so they could get back to their original mission: *"You are witnesses of these things."* Imagine all of the other responses Jesus could have made in this situation. He could have employed shame, guilt, duty, obligation, command, brow-beating, etc. But he knew two things: their hearts were fragile, and they had to rediscover Jesus, the risen Christ.

We see Jesus using the power of questions, deep listening, support, encouragement, and the skill of guiding these disciples back onto their critical path. We could say more about Jesus's ability to listen, but the fact is self-evident. No one listened more intently to people than Jesus. Listening values the person who is doing the talking. It honors their existence as nothing else can do. Asking and listening demonstrate that we believe in the other person. Notice that Jesus didn't tell the men to do anything. There are no commands in this story, no "should-have," "you'd better or else," "shame on you," or any number of other tactics we often use to get people to do what we want them to.

Jesus challenged these disciples to do what they had already committed to doing. And then He asked them whether they had anything to eat. In fact, it was during the course of their common meal that their eyes were opened and they recognized that Jesus Himself had been talking to them. But first He used open-ended questions and listening to help them get unstuck and gain a fresh perspective, based on the truth. Then he offered them encouragement to reengage with their heart's true desire: *"to be witnesses of these things."* That's good coaching!

2. The second story is found in John 21, and it involves Peter, the leader of the disciples. This story is similar to the first in that it demonstrates how Jesus "coached" his disciples to redirect their thoughts and actions. As the story opens we find Peter, their leader, leading the disciples back to fishing, not forward into their assigned mission. Let's see how Jesus responds.

Jesus had instructed the disciples to wait for Him at the Sea of Galilee, but they were growing weary of waiting. What happens to us in that kind of situation? We start looking around for Plan B. For the disciples, Plan B involved going back to what they knew best—fishing. Peter says simply, *"I'm going out to fish."* The others respond, *"We'll go with you."* But a problem emerges: try as they might, they don't catch anything.

Jesus enters the story from the shadows on the shore with what some see as a humorously obvious rhetorical question: *Friends* [*Children* in some translations], *haven't you any fish?* They had been distracted away from their critical path, and Jesus was inviting them to think more deeply about the implications of their decision. Jesus, the Master Fisher of Men, was about to gently "reel them in."

The way in which Jesus helps them change their perspectives and direction is intriguing. First, he redirects their fishing efforts to the other side of the boat, and they experience remarkable success. This is a "follow Me" teachable moment, but it takes a while for them to begin to grasp its significance. Then the disciple "whom Jesus loved" tells Peter, *"It is the Lord,"* and the coach approach begins to bear fruit. For one thing, Jesus cooks them a good breakfast and invites them to join Him on shore. Hospitality breaks down barriers. We can be sure that He listened intently to their conversation around the early morning fire and watched their body language; they no doubt squirmed a bit under His penetrating gaze. But Jesus never reprimanded them, never condemned their behavior or their motives. He didn't resort to guilt or shame to beat them back into shape. Instead, He showed them genuine hospitality and gave them the gift of his listening and loving presence. Jesus coached.

It's amazing to read how Jesus engages Peter, the presumed leader who had so recently misled the disciples away from their mission and back to fishing. What would you have said to Peter? What do you think Peter was expecting Jesus to say? This is probably the first time Jesus and Peter had spoken to one another after Peter's three denials just before Jesus's crucifixion. If you had been Peter, what would have expected? Probably something like "Wow, Peter, way to go! What do you mean you don't know me? How could you have said such a stupid thing? You're not a leader but a coward; the crowing of that rooster proved it! I don't think you have what it takes to follow me. I've had enough of you. You're fired."

But Jesus took a completely different tack; He took the *coach approach*. He asked an honest question that went to the heart of what Peter needed to grapple with. After all, love was at the center of Jesus's relationship with His disciples, and Peter knew it. Jesus asked a simple, probing question: *"Peter, do you love me?"* He didn't accuse Peter of anything. He didn't penalize him for his denials. He didn't cut his pay. He didn't suspend him from the team. He didn't scold him for being a bad influence on the rest of the disciples. He simply invited him back into a right relationship by going to the heart of the issue. If love covers a multitude of sins, then for sure it covered Peter's denials. All three of them. If the blood of the Messiah poured out on the Jerusalem garbage dump really was the full atonement for the sin of the world, then Peter could confidently come clean before Jesus and tell him the truth. And the truth was that Peter really did love Jesus. How do we know? Because Jesus reinstated Peter, accepted his answers, and recommissioned him with his original call: *"Follow me."*

And Peter did follow Jesus. All the way to a martyr's death, so we're told by the historian Josephus. Evidence of Peter's transformation can be found when, many years later, Peter himself wrote, *"Humble yourselves, therefore, under God's mighty hand, that he may lift you up in due time. Cast all your anxiety on him because he cares for you"* (1 Peter 5:6–7). Where do you think Peter learned that? During breakfast on the beach? In that talk with Jesus after breakfast? If so, that was true life transformation, facilitated by the coach approach that characterized Jesus's entire ministry.

Both of these stories are profound examples of the power of coaching: asking, listening, guiding, supporting, encouraging, and holding people accountable. Receiving information and advice does not cause transformation. Real inner change requires renewal from within, as the apostle Paul reminds us . . .

"Do not conform to the pattern of this world, but be transformed by the renewing of your mind. Then you will be able to test and approve what God's will is—his good, pleasing and perfect will." —Romans 12:2

Is coaching biblical? Can we find examples of it in the Bible? Can we find the *coach approach* being used in Jesus's ministry? We believe so. What do you think?

 ## The Coach asks . . .

- If instead of asking questions to obtain information you began using questions to help others think through the challenges they face, as Jesus did, how might those individuals benefit?

- What have you learned so far about how asking questions instead of giving advice guides people to make better choices?

- What have you learned so far about how coaching can help people discover those "good works" that God has prepared in advance for them to do?

- Read once again through the questions Jesus asked. Do you hear Him asking any of those questions of you? If so, how will you answer?

O Read on.

4

COACHING WORKS!

The term *coach* emerged in the world of sports in the late 1800s, and that remains the image that comes to mind for many when coaching is mentioned. This is unfortunate because the type of coaching generally practiced in the world of sports is the exact opposite of what we mean by *coaching*.

Sports coaching focuses on telling athletes and teams how to play the game. It takes place in a command and control setting, and too often those portrayed as the "best" coaches are characterized by an in-your-face, I'll tell you what to do and how to do it, my way or the highway style. From continuously observing those images we grow to assume that the best results are achieved through using those techniques.

It's interesting to note that, according to many in the coaching profession today, W. T. Gallwey's 1974 book, *The Inner Game of Tennis*, represents the first major effort to transition from focusing on how the game should be played to coaching individuals and groups to define and pursue the specific goals they wish to achieve. Sir John Whitmore, British racing driver and sports psychologist, stated, "Gallwey was the first to demonstrate a simple and comprehensive method of coaching that could be readily applied to almost any situation" (J. Whitmore, *Coaching for Performance*, 1992, p. 7).

In ministry we tend to lean heavily on the "I'll tell you what to do and how to do it" model. The emphasis is on dispensing information and advice, expecting that if we give people enough of the "right" stuff they will change. We call this the "spray and pray" approach—spray as much information and advice on the wall as you can and pray that something will stick. When people do not change and respond in the way we had hoped, we are disappointed. "Why don't they do what we told or taught them to do?" we ask. It's because those we sought to help didn't become internally motivated to change.

Coaching has the power and potential to give us the results we seek, and there is substantial evidence to support the claim that *coaching works!*

Evaluating the Impact of Coaching

Turning to the coaching profession, we discover that essentially three methods are used to evaluate and measure the impact of coaching.

1. The *Level of Satisfaction* expressed by those being coached. Interviews and surveys are used during and following coaching to find out ways in which those being coached feel they have benefited from the experience. Those benefits are typically expressed in terms of personal growth and performance improvement.

2. Observed and, where possible, measured *Improvements in Attitudes and Performance*. The focus is on real and

tangible changes that benefit both the organization and the individual being coached. Measured results are typically expressed as the percentage of those being coaching who were observed as having, or who reported, a specific attitudinal or behavioral change.

3. *Return on Investment.* The value of coaching is measured by revenue increases and/or cost reductions produced by those being coached, as compared to the money and time invested in coaching. This is a tricky area, and the various Coaching ROI formulas being used tend to be controversial.

Studies on the Impact of Coaching

The following four studies contain a mix of the above evaluation methods. Each provides clear evidence that coaching works in a variety of situations. As you explore these studies, keep asking *why*—Why does coaching work? And then ask *how*—How might these benefits apply to the ministries that are important to me?

1. This first study included 100 executives, mostly from Fortune 1000 companies, who were coached by professional Executive Coaches from Manchester, Inc. This is believed to be the first major study to quantify the business impact of coaching. Here is a summary of the findings.

   • They realized an average Return on Investment (ROI) of 5.7 times the cost of the coaching.

   • The percentage of those being coached who reported the following performance improvements were: productivity (53%), quality (48%), customer service (39%), cost reductions (23%), bottom-line profitability (22%).

- Personal benefits reported: improved working relationships with direct reports (77%), improved working relationships with immediate supervisor (71%), better teamwork (67%), conflict reduction (52%), higher organizational commitment (44%), improved working relationships with clients (37%)

("Maximizing the Impact of Executive Coaching: Behavioral Change, Organizational Outcomes, and Return on Investment," *The Manchester Review*, Vol. 6, No. 1, 2001.)

2. Next is a study by Clear Coaching, conducted from October to December 2006. The survey was completed by 30 retail companies, all of which had employed coaches for their employees over the years. Here is what they found.
   - Of the companies documented, 23% reported increases in sales and revenue, even when this wasn't a specific goal of the coaching. The other 63% did not measure financial return. The conclusion was that companies could be gaining tangible financial benefits from coaching without even realizing it.
   - The following shows the percentage of companies that identified each of the tangible results from coaching: acquired a new skill or improved an existing one (50%), improved team working relationships (50%), increased motivation (43%), improved work performance (43%), changed approaches to improve work situations (37%).

(Julia Marber, *Are There Any Tangible Benefits to Coaching? Are There Any Positive Financial Returns? Survey Results*, Clear Coaching Ltd., February 2007.)

3. The authors of this study measured the impact of coaching on 31 managers in a US city health agency. In phase one, all of the managers participated in a three-day, classroom-style training workshop that focused on their work roles. The participants rated the training workshop very high on all quantitative and qualitative measures.

   In phase two, the 31 managers were provided with eight weeks of coaching that was focused on helping them apply what they had learned in the training workshop.

   The authors found that while their training program increased manager productivity of those not coached by an average of 22%, adding the eight weeks of coaching following the training increased productivity for the 31 managers an average of 88%.

   (G. Olivero, K. D. Bane, and R. E. Kopelman, "Executive Coaching as a Transfer of Training Tool: Effects on Productivity in a Public Agency," *Public Personnel Management*, Winter 1997.)

4. This study comes from Ute Kueffner, who works as a program manager and coach in the corporate university of a global software company. It focuses on a pilot sales development program that included the following.

   • A two-day coaching workshop for sales managers, focusing on generic coaching skills and on how to coach sales negotiation effectiveness.

   • Professional coaching for managers, helping them apply a coaching style in their daily work and to foster their own growth.

   • Managers coaching their account executives (sale people) to help them improve sales negotiation effectiveness.

At the beginning of the program, account executives rated their sales negotiation skills and, together with their managers, defined the coaching focus and desired outcome of the coaching.

The impact of the coaching was evaluated three months later. Sales managers and account executives unanimously agreed that the coaching had impacted their behavior and the business results they achieved. They were able to shorten the sales cycle, generate more opportunities, and grow bigger deals. The overall results were tremendous compared to the program costs of $60,000.

(Ute Kueffner, *Better Business Results Through Coaching*, 2005.)

Why Does Coaching Work?

The above case studies focus on documenting the results of coaching. But those results don't simply happen. They evolve over time from what occurs in the coaching process. You'll learn more about that in the next section, where we answer the question "What is it like to be coached?" Meanwhile, here is an example from Bill (not his real name) that occurred early in his professional coaching career.

In order to coach professionally full time, you need clients. When I began, I was much more prepared to coach than I was to build a coaching practice. So, I hired a business development coach.

After our second or third coaching conversation, we started talking about the size and quality of my network—and my willingness and ability to use networking as a client attraction strategy. As I was determining how that strategy would work for me, my coach said, "Let's talk about setting a new client attraction goal." Here is part of the conversation that followed.

Coach: How many full-time clients would you like to coach every week?

Me: I'd like to have 10; I really need 10 clients to make it financially.

Coach: How many new clients do you believe you can bring in over the next 30 days?

Me: I think I can commit to 6 new clients.

Coach: After listening to you talk about how much you enjoy networking, I want to challenge you to increase that to 10.

I accepted his challenge and increased my goal to 10 new clients in 30 days. It was not an easy commitment to make, but I was bolstered by my coach's confidence in me, and by the networking strategy I had established.

So, how did I do? Thirty days later, I had 11 new clients, and two months later, I had 21. Each week, my coach and I talked about what I had done, what worked, what didn't work, and the adjustments I needed to make during the next week of networking. Things happened over those two months, but I realized the importance of defining exactly what I needed to do and following the daily action steps that I knew would help me achieve my goal.

Successful people do what unsuccessful people are unwilling to do, and being coached will help you better understand the difference.

Two of the studies documented significant improvements in performance when coaching followed training. It wasn't because of poor training. It was because coaching helped each individual translate learning into doing and provided a supportive process that enabled the person being coached to sustain that doing over time. It's also clear that each individual had defined and was pursuing goals they wanted to achieve. They were empowered to take ownership of and responsibility for shaping their own future. Note also the reported improvements in relationship areas—improved teamwork, better relations with clients and supervisors, and higher organizational commitment.

 ## The Coach asks . . .

- Reflecting back on Bill's early coaching experience, why do you think he was willing to commit to bringing in only six new clients in thirty days when he knew he needed ten?

- Continuing with Bill, how would you explain the role coaching played in enabling him to actually attract twenty-one new clients within two months?

- The average improvement of 88% versus 22% achieved by coached managers in the public agency is worth noting. What if you could experience that level of improvement in your ministry efforts? What would that look like? What impact would that have? How would it make you feel?

- Think about a specific ministry in your church, if possible one in which you are involved . How would that ministry benefit from improvements in the areas reported in the first study above: improved working relationships, better teamwork, conflict reduction, higher organizational commitment, and improved working relationships with clients?

◉ Read on.

5

WHO BENEFITS MOST FROM COACHING?

The answer to the Who benefits? question transcends age, gender, nationality, stage of life, profession, or any other category into which we typically place people. The reality is this . . .

- Anyone *can benefit* from coaching, but not everyone *will benefit* from it.
- Coaching is for those who *want to change* and believe that coaching is the best way to get the help they need to make that change.

Back in Chapter 2 we saw how a nine-year boy old benefitted from being coached by his grandmother. How did that happen? The answer lies in his response to the first question his grandmother asked . . .

Me: Is there anything you long to do or accomplish? What would that look like?

Him: OH! I'd like to collect a thousand Pokémon cards! You mean like that?

Looking at his desire to collect Pokémon cards, he determined that he was not where he wanted to be. He was ready to be coached, and his grandmother confirmed his desire to close the gap with this question . . .

"How might you go about building your collection? How could we close the gap of where you are right now, having no cards, and where you want to be, having 1,000 cards?"

He was hooked, and ready to be coached.

Ready to Be Coached

When pondering the various aspects of their life, most people can identify specific areas where they can say Where I am is not where I want to be. They think about it; they talk about it; they may even ask a friend or two, "What do you think I should do?" But that's as far as it goes. There are several reasons why this happens.

- They have become comfortable with the status quo; it's familiar territory. Doing something about it would push them further outside their comfort zone than they are willing to go.
- They haven't made doing something about it a high enough priority at this point.
- They struggle with *paralysis of analysis*. Before they can make a significant change, they need to read and study and prepare over and over again.
- The people closest to them are not very supportive.
- The answers they got to their "What do you think I should do?" question haven't been helpful—or they've

felt overwhelmed by the magnitude of what people have suggested.

- There's this little voice in the recesses of their mind that keeps saying "Are you crazy? You can't do this! What would people say? You're better off not trying that. Just keep doing what you're doing, and you'll be OK." Many in the coaching profession refer to this voice as the Gremlin on your shoulder.

These are challenging obstacles to overcome, and rarely are we able to break through solely on our own. The good news is that coaching can empower you to close that gap—or any gap. Two things need to happen.

- The desire to change and close that gap must become stronger than the fear and hesitation that keep us from taking that step. Closing that gap must become a top priority.
- We need to understand what coaching does and believe that it is through being coached that we have the best opportunity to achieve our goal.

Coaching is a process whereby our efforts to close that gap build over time. Readiness to be coached also means eagerness to engage in that process with a person we can depend on to guide us toward our goal.

What to Expect

Here's what you can expect from your coach as you begin the coaching process.

- Your coach will ask lots of questions to help you think through issues and options and to guide you in making wise choices.
- At some point your coach will ask you to say specifically what it is you want to accomplish.
- You will be asked to set the agenda for each coaching conversation.
- Your coach will assure you that everything said will be kept confidential, and you will find that he or she honors that promise.
- You will discover that your coach never judges what you say or decide.
- You will constantly be encouraged to step up and step out.
- At the end of each coaching conversation, your coach will ask what action steps you wish to take between then and the next time you meet.

The bottom line in coaching is *change.* Coaching is for those who no longer want things to remain the same. Knowing what to expect, they see that coaching can help them make change happen. Here are a few examples from our own coaching experience.

- A friend of Tim's approached him one day and said, "I'm going to retire in a few years, and I don't have a clue about God's purpose for my future. I have to figure this out. I don't want to drift through retirement being in the same place year after year." They began a coaching relationship, and within several months he and his wife had discovered enough about their identity, passion, and values to design a mission and vision for their future. Instead of dreading retirement, they began to look forward to what God had planned for them.

- A couple that Mike and his wife had known for years was visiting. They were celebrating the husband's retirement after having served for more than forty years as a pastor. He was celebrating, but it soon became clear that his wife was not as happy about it as he was. There were a number of things she missed, but most important were the opportunities she had enjoyed to play the piano in worship and for other activities. It was clear that she wanted to find new outlets but didn't know where to start. Mike offered to coach her by phone when they returned home. She agreed. During the first call Mike discovered two issues. One was finding new outlets, and the other was her fear that she would have to learn lots of new music. During the next five weeks Mike was able to help her determine how she could overcome both obstacles. She soon discovered that as she found new opportunities, her desire to learn new music began to push aside her fears. Mike helped her deal with that by having her clarify a technique she could use to learn a new song. It wasn't long before music had once again become a significant part of her life.

When you want to change you are faced with two challenges: determining what you need to do, and doing it. Coaching empowers you to do both.

The Coach asks . . .

- Select an aspect of your life of which you can say "Where I am is not where I want to be." What needs to change?

- Under the heading *Ready to be Coached,* there is a list of six reasons people resist change. As you think about the "What needs to change?" question, do any of those reasons apply to you?

- Under the heading *What To Expect,* there is a list of seven ways in which a skilled coach will help you close the "Where I am is not where I want to be" gap. How might that coaching experience help you overcome the reason(s) you selected?

▶ Read on.

WHAT IS IT LIKE TO BE COACHED?

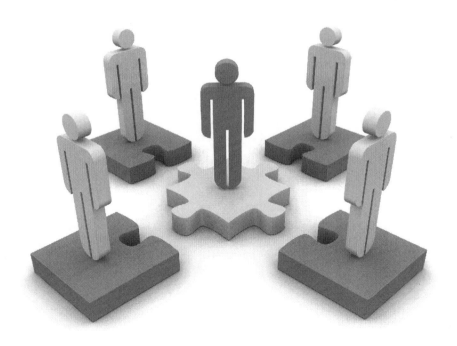

6

COACHING IS NOT THE SAME AS . . . ANYTHING!

There's nothing quite like it—*coaching*, that is. And there's a good reason we say that.

Other familiar approaches to spiritual transformation, personal growth, and leader development rely on having experts impart their knowledge, wisdom, and advice to us. We can certainly benefit from that, but simply receiving helpful information and good advice does nothing to ensure that we will do anything with it.

As we intake new information, we are internally wrestling with three questions.

- *What* does it all mean?
- *Why* is it important to me?
- *How* will I use it in my daily life?

Also known as the "What?, So What?, Now What?" reflective learning process (G. Rolfe, D. Freshwater , and M. Jasper, *Critical Reflection in Nursing and the Helping Professions: a User's Guide*, Basingstoke: Palgrave Macmillan; 2001), these questions represent the conclusions we need to make before we become willing to exert the effort to use what we have learned. The expert up front or sitting across the table from us typically feels compelled to answer those three questions for us, relying on their eloquence and powers of persuasion to convince us to take action. But change doesn't come that easily.

Coaching takes a totally different approach.

Coaching is based on the principle that the people you coach will understand, value, and apply what you help them discover for themselves—not what you tell them.

Coaching is a question-guided, self-discovery process that produces action.

Imagine that you have been thinking about a specific, important area of your life. You've reached the point at which you've decided, "Where I am is not where I want to be—and I'm ready to get help with closing that gap."

You have several "get help" options.

- Friendly or "expert" advice
- Mentoring
- Teaching/training
- Coaching

We are going to explore the first three options by contrasting each with coaching. Then we'll look at two others that are often mentioned: *counseling/therapy* and *consulting*.

Friendly/Expert Advice versus Coaching

- When you go to someone for friendly or expert advice, you begin by sharing the details of your situation. It isn't long before they begin telling you what they believe you should do.

- In contrast, when you share the details of your situation with your coach, they immediately begin asking questions that help you discover and decide where you want to go, how you plan to get there, and what you will do in the next week to move in the direction of accomplishing your goal.

Mentoring versus Coaching

- Having been in your situation, a mentor provides guidance, direction, and even career advice when it's appropriate.

- On the other hand, your coach asks you about your experience and helps you set goals and harness that experience to achieve those goals.

Teaching/Training versus Coaching

- Whether in a classroom setting or one-on-one, your teacher/trainer focuses on presenting new information and using various "hands-on" techniques to help you learn new skills.

- Your coach focuses on helping you apply the knowledge and skills you already have (or are presently learning) toward achieving the goals you have set. In Chapter 4, the third example describes a city health agency in which 31 managers received eight weeks of coaching following three days of training. Their productivity increased on an average of 88%, as compared to 22% for those managers who did not receive coaching following the training.

Gaining new information, insights, guidance, and skills through processes other than coaching definitely has value. What's often missing, however, is the creation of concrete action steps that enable you to apply what the experts are trying to impart.

The fact is that you haven't learned anything until you use it, evaluate the results, make adjustments, and use it again.

This *learning cycle* is an integral part of the coaching process, and everything is focused on helping you close the gap between where you are and where you want to be.

What about *counseling/therapy* and *consulting*? How do they differ?

Counseling/Therapy versus Coaching

- One of the difficulties in making this comparison is that counselors/therapists provide a wide range of services. Some focus on issues of pathology, healing, and unresolved psychological issues of the past. Those who practice solution-focused therapy are more present/future oriented, but their focus is still on personal problems that need to be solved. The overall emphasis is that the client needs help or a cure. Counselors/therapists are experts in the problems their clients bring to them. It's interesting to note that as coaching becomes better understood, a growing number of counselors/therapists are adding this skill to their list of services. Some are even transitioning their counseling practice to a coaching practice.

- Your coach is not an expert in solving the particular challenge you face. He or she is a person with a set of coaching skills to help you set and pursue your own goals, explore options, make wise choices, overcome obstacles, and celebrate your achievements. Your coach helps you set goals in the present and take ownership of your future.

Consulting versus Coaching

- Consultants generally specialize in business processes, technology, or management/employee development. They are hired for their expertise. Typically a consultant will analyze the problems they have been called in to address and then propose a plan of action. They may or may not be involved in the implementation of that plan.
- When coaching is involved, the person being coached is the expert. Your coach empowers you to take control of and responsibility for defining and pursuing the future you want.

The difference between coaching and all of these other expert-driven processes boils down to one vital factor: coaching empowers you to change without telling you what you should do.

The Coach asks . . .

- What has been your experience when asking someone else for advice? How often have you done specifically what they said you should do?

- When you attend a class, workshop, or seminar, what percentage of the information and advice presented do you typically go home and use in your daily life?

- What enables you to apply more of what you gain from coaching than you typically would with the other "get help" options?

- What does "empowered to change" mean to you? Why is it important?

O Read on.

STRIVING FOR A FULFILLED AND BALANCED LIFE

Most of us sense that there is a more meaningful and productive way we could live our lives. We periodically ask "How could _____ be better than it is?" Depending on what has occurred recently to bring that question to mind, we might fill in the blank with any number of things.

- My job and career
- My spiritual life
- My health
- My finances
- My relationship with my family
- The way I spend my spare time

This question expresses our desire to experience greater *fulfillment* in key areas of our life. On the surface, this may sound like a search for more stuff or the desire to simply feel good about something. But there's more to it than that. More *stuff* and *good feelings* bring temporary satisfaction at best. Our sense of true fulfillment is rooted in our values and our search for life purpose.

As Ephesians 2:10 reminds us, *"We are God's handiwork, created in Christ Jesus to do good works, which God prepared in advance for us to do."* That's not simply an interesting passage; it's a promise. And it expresses exactly what we are searching for. Discovering and living out those *"good works, which God prepared in advance for us to do"* constitute the *real stuff* that defines true fulfillment in each aspect of our life.

In our busy and chaotic pace of daily living, we also periodically complain about the lack of **balance** in our life. As we think about one or more areas where we sense a lack of fulfillment, we recognize that some aspects of our life are receiving more of our attention than others. And we feel guilty about that.

Balance is never static; it's always a moving target. We are continually moving either toward balance or away from it. When we do nothing about unfulfilled areas, we are moving away from balance. But once we begin doing something to experience greater fulfillment in one or more of these important areas, we move toward balance—and feel better about ourselves and our situation.

Coaching for Fulfillment and Life Balance

Coaching takes place in the context of our desire to seek greater fulfillment and balance in our life. Many coaches use a tool called the **Wheel of Life** to help people define the area(s) in which they want to be coached.

The **Wheel of Life** illustrates *life balance*, which is in turn influenced by the *sense of fulfillment* the individual is experiencing in each category included on the wheel. The labels used here represent typical, general categories for an average adult.

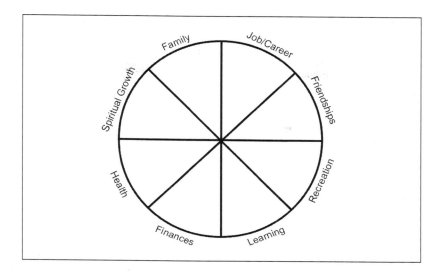

Any set of meaningful labels can be used. The fourth *impact of coaching* study found in Chapter 4 states that a two-day coaching workshop for sales managers was conducted "focusing on . . . how to coach sales negotiation effectiveness." It wasn't mentioned there, but a **Wheel of Life** using that set of "sales negotiation effectiveness" factors was used with the sales force to define where they needed the most help.

Viewing the center as *0 Fulfillment* and the outer edge of the circle as *100 percent Fulfillment,* the person being coached is asked to draw a line in each category indicating the *percentage of Fulfillment* they believe they are currently experiencing in that category.

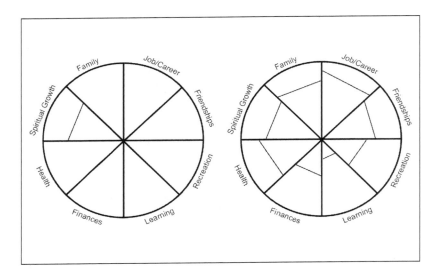

When introducing the **Wheel of Life** as a coaching tool in our *Empowerment Coaching Training*, we expand the exercise this way . . .

- Place a checkmark (✓) inside each category in which you can identify specific areas that are holding you back.
- Select specific areas of which you can say, "Where I am not is not where I want to be, and I could use some help in closing that gap."

The folks at MindTools.com call this "taking a helicopter view of your life so you can bring things back into balance." Following the instructions above, you can use the **Wheel of Life** to explore life as you experience it.

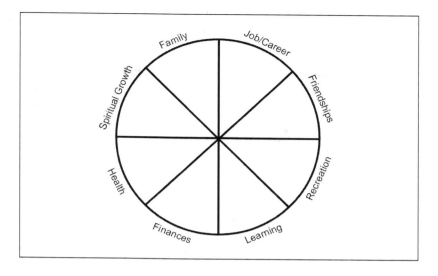

If you were sitting across the table from someone who agreed to coach you, what would you tell him or her is the area in which you would most like to close the gap between where you are now and where you would like to be?

Once you answer that question, you are ready to begin the coaching experience.

 ## The Coach asks . . .

- Select one of the **Wheel of Life** areas. What would being more *fulfilled* in that area look and feel like to you?

- As you begin to take specific steps to becoming more *fulfilled* in that area, how will you benefit on a daily basis?

- As you begin to experience those benefits, how will they impact you sense of *life balance*?

◗ **Read on.**

8

THE COACHING EXPERIENCE

The mission of the Empowerment Coaching Network is to bring Christ-centered peer coaching to the church. We emphasize *peer* coaching because we believe that anyone who cares about helping others will benefit greatly from learning how to coach.

A *coaching experience* does not have to be prearranged. After you have learned how to coach, a casual conversation can easily evolve into a coaching conversation whenever you sense that the person you are talking with is telling you that where they are is not where they want to be. For example, imagine a conversation that goes like this . . .

You: Hi, Ruth. How was your week?

Ruth: To tell you the truth, my week has not been all that great.

You: I'm sorry to hear that. What happened?

This conversation could continue as a causal exchange with a friend. But if Ruth's response to this last question suggests that there are one or more issues troubling her, you could decide to begin probing to see whether there is an issue or obstacle she might want to resolve. After listening to "what happened," you would ask a question such as

> If you could identify one issue you would like to resolve, what would that be?

Assuming that Ruth does identify that issue, you could then ask

> Could you expand on that?

You have now made the shift from a casual to a coaching conversation, probably without Ruth recognizing what has occurred. However, once you have been coaching for a while, and people become aware of it, some may sense when that shift has occurred.

This happened to Mike soon after he began professional coaching. He had joined a Business Networking International (BNI) group to help build his coaching practice. One of the requirements of BNI is to arrange meetings with other members to learn more about what they do so you can refer prospective customers to them. Mike was engaged in such a meeting in a coffee shop, and the woman with whom he was meeting told him that she was considering returning to school to pursue a new career direction. Mike began asking probing questions to learn more and help her think through some of the issues she was facing. Suddenly, she looked at Mike and asked "You're coaching me, aren't you!"

Once that initial conversation draws to an end, you might sense the need to continue helping Ruth with what you have been discussing. So you ask, "Would you like to continue talking about this?" If she says yes, you can determine where and when you will meet. Note that all of this has occurred without either of you ever mentioning coaching.

The Coaching Conversation

The *coaching conversation* typically begins with your coach asking a casual but probing question to simply get the conversation going and find out what is going on in your life.

"How was your week?"

"What's going on in your life these days?"

"What would you like to talk about?"

Then, instead of giving you friendly or "expert" advice about something you said, your coach will ask PROBING questions to help you explore and better understand the situation and issues you have raised.

What aspect of that situation are you most eager to change?

How would you describe the GAP between where you are now and where you want to be?

What obstacles do you believe are standing in the way of closing that gap?

What was your most important accomplishment since you began that project?

What have you learned from that experience?

What options do you see for making the changes you want?

Your coach has been trained to coach moment by moment, never trying to anticipate what you will say next. Instead, he or she is listening for the insights you have gained from your experiences, for key events and turning points in your life, and for patterns of thinking that guide your actions.

If you ask "What do you think I should do?" your coach will respond with a question such as

What do you see as your options in this situation?

Frequently, your coach will follow probing questions with EXPANDING questions to broaden your thinking.

What else did you learn from that experience?

What other courses of action can you think of?

What have you seen others do that might work here?

What would a five look like in that area? What about a ten?

As you think further about this, what else comes to mind?

And then your coach will use CLOSURE questions to help you make wise choices and take action.

What specifically would you like to accomplish?

Which option do you believe will best achieve the objectives you have set?

After you have responded to the "What specifically would you like to accomplish?" question, your coach will help you establish a measurable and achievable goal that will pull you toward closing that gap between where you are now and where you want to be.

What is your timeline for achieving this goal?

What are you currently doing to achieve this goal? What's working? What isn't working?

What specific activities do you need to accomplish each week in order to achieve your goal?

Then, at the end of each coaching conversation, your coach will ask you what actions you want to take that will move you closer to your goal before your next scheduled meeting.

What is your top priority for this week?

What specific action do you want to take between now and our next meeting?

When will you have that completed—and how will I know?

Here is an example from Angelyn, who describes her first attempt at coaching right after completing our *Empowerment Coaching Training*.

My daughter, a junior in college, had some important decisions to make regarding her next school year. She called to talk about it. Little did she know that I had just completed coaching training . . . so I did some "stealth" coaching in our conversation to practice my new skills.

It was really amazing! First of all, I noticed that I was a more intentional listener, and that meant my questions (still using my notebook because we were on the phone!) were more meaningful and relevant. It gave her an opportunity to really explore her own thoughts and ideas in a way that she couldn't do on her own with everything all "bottled up" in her head.

Throughout the conversation, she was able to see some "holes" in the information and ideas she held. She processed where she was stuck and began to see what her next step needed to be. She left our conversation with an "action plan" of her own making—not mine, or influenced by me as may have previously been the case.

When we said goodbye, she said, "Thanks Mom, this has been really helpful." (YES!) She still doesn't know that

I've taken the coaching training, but she has called me a couple more times to help her talk/think through some other situations. This is precisely why I took the class. I knew it would come in handy in conversations with my kids and family. I promise to tell her (someday) that I took the training, but for now I'll let her think that I'm just naturally an awesome mom who asks great questions.

Go to your favorite Internet search engine and enter the phrase "benefits of coaching." As you explore the entries that appear, you will discover a number of quotes from people and organizations who have discovered the power of the coaching experience. Here are a few.

"I never cease to be amazed at the power of the coaching process to draw out the skills or talent that was previously hidden within an individual, and which invariably finds a way to solve a problem previously thought unsolvable." —John Russell, Managing Director, Harley-Davidson Europe Ltd.

"I absolutely believe that people, unless coached, never reach their full potential." —Bob Nardelli, CEO, Home Depot

"He asked deep, thought-provoking questions that once I discovered the answer, I could embark on the course of action exactly right for me. I have avoided many traps, and I have prioritized key decisions and positioned my business at a much higher level than I would have without his help." —D. W., Asheville, North Carolina

We believe that coaching is for anyone who wants to grow, and that anyone who wants to help others grow can learn to coach. It's as simple as that.

The Coach asks . . .

We're going to focus on the three quotations above.

- John Russell suggests that coaching draws out the skills or talent previously hidden within an individual. How do you think coaching accomplishes that?

- How might coaching enable a person to solve a problem previously thought unsolvable?

- How might coaching enable a person to achieve more of their potential?

- What benefits of coaching sited by D. W. have you thinking "I'd sure like to be able to say that"?

O Read on.

9

BUILDING MINISTRY THROUGH COACHING

It wasn't that long ago that *ministry* was believed to be the work done by "church professionals"—pastors, evangelists, missionaries, or leaders of faith-based parachurch organizations. We take a more holistic view these days. Ministry now includes all those involved in organized efforts to build the Body of Christ and reach the world for Christ, whether within the context of a local church, denominational agency, or parachurch organization. There is even a point of view that suggests that ministry should be expanded to include every believer in every occupation, regardless of where they are employed.

Our focus here is on those organized efforts to build the Body of Christ and reach the world for Christ, whether they occur in a local church or in a faith-based parachurch organizational setting. Our question is this: How can we build ministry through coaching? To answer it, we first need to understand what ministry is all about.

Ministry Is . . .

We understand ministry as service to God, performed to glorify Christ. The Greek word in the New Testament that is often translated as "ministry" is *diakonia*, which means "to serve."

- To serve—*"So Christ himself gave the apostles, the prophets, the evangelists, the pastors and teachers, to equip his people for works of service"*— Ephesians 4:11–12
- To glorify Christ—*"Whatever you do, work at it with all your heart, as working for the Lord, not for human masters, since you know that you will receive an inheritance from the Lord as a reward. It is the Lord Christ you are serving."* —Colossians 3:23–24

A Framework for Understanding Ministry

Ministries today come in many flavors. Defining a framework for understanding ministry is no simple task, but we believe it is well worth the effort to do so. Here goes! What follows will hopefully create a balance for you between *all-encompassing* and *easy to understand.*

Categories of Ministry

Place	Church		Parachurch	
Reach	In	Out	Up	Down
Structure	Age		Target Group	

1. **Place**
   - Church—A ministry of a local church.
   - Parachurch—The ministry of a faith-based parachurch organization.

2. **Reach**
   - In—Reaching those inside the church through fellowship, encouragement, accountability, and other Body building and edifying ministries.
   - Out—Reaching those outside the church through evangelism, missions, and various types of help and care ministries.
   - Up—Uniting believers in community and giving to God through worship, prayer, and praising ministries.
   - Down—God revealing Himself through Bible study and various other teaching ministries.
   - (Our thanks to Seth Honeycutt, who originated this section of our model and placed it in the public domain for all to enjoy.)

3. **Structure**
   - Age—Ministries focusing on a specific age range, such as children's worship for ages four through six.
   - Target Group—Ministries organized to reach a group identified by a specific mix of age, gender, interests, and/or common characteristics. Examples: youth group, boys' club, seniors, widows, single parents . . . the list is almost endless.

Creating a Model for Your Ministry

A key challenge is to avoid allowing ministries to become *programs* where those involved simply follow a program script week after week, forgetting that ministry is a calling to serve God by serving others in the name of Jesus Christ. That requires us to see our ministry as a *process*—which we defined in the Introduction as "meeting people where they are and taking them to where God wants them to be."

It is worth stepping back and reevaluating, and possibly redefining, your ministry in terms that will enable you to avoid the program trap. Here is a way to build a model for your ministry that can help you do that . . .

1. **Focus**—Identify the *Place*, *Reach*, and *Structure* of your ministry.
   - Have you clearly defined the *Place*, *Reach*, and *Structure* of your ministry?
   - Does your present "label" for this ministry accurately reflect that focus? If not, consider giving it a new label.

2. **Purpose**—Determine why this ministry is important.
   - Who is this ministry intended to reach? Why?
   - How do you strive to serve God and glorify Christ in this ministry?

3. **Process**—Identify how you will achieve your purpose.
   - How will you "meet people where they are and take them to where God wants them to be?"
   - What is your "take them" process?
   - What steps will you take to prevent this ministry from evolving into a routine program?

4. **Outcome**—Clearly understand the results you hope and pray God will enable you to achieve.
   - What are those results?
   - How will you monitor and measure them?

Building Your Ministry through Coaching

To build a ministry, you need people who meet two criteria.
- They share the vision that drives your *Ministry Model.*
- They are equipped for their role in that ministry.

Every ministry needs persons to serve in three distinct roles.
- Someone who *coordinates* the ministry with the other ministries of that church or organization.
- Someone who *leads* the ministry.
- People who *do* the ministry.

If coordinating, leading, and doing your ministry are characterized solely by efforts to impart knowledge, wisdom, and advice to others, the outcome you achieve will be seriously limited. There are two reasons for that.
- No one can have the knowledge, wisdom, and expert advice that is required for all of the situations they will encounter. Feeling the pressure to respond, those they seek to serve will too often fail to receive what they really need.
- Regardless of the role you occupy, the process of your ministry must involve taking people "where God wants them to be." *"For we are God's handiwork, created in Christ Jesus to do good works, which God prepared in advance for us to do"* (Ephesians 2:10). We cannot possibly know on

behalf of someone else precisely what those "good works" need to be, and we certainly cannot know where God wants each individual to be.

As we stated in the Introduction, we believe that coaching is the single most effective process for guiding spiritual transformation, personal growth, and leader development. Coaching works because it empowers people to change without telling them what they should do. Coaching helps people discover where God wants them to be, helping people to take responsibility for defining and pursuing their own future. Here is how that works for each of the three roles identified above.

- **Ministry Coordinator**—By coaching the leaders of the various ministries he or she coordinates, this individual ensures that those leaders become empowered to define and shape the future of that ministry. Through the experience of being coached, they also have a model to follow in guiding the others involved in the ministry they lead.

- **Ministry Leader**—By coaching the people they lead in their ministry, these individuals empower them to take whatever they already know and are learning about the ministry and apply it to their ministry efforts in ways that have meaning and value to them. Through the experience of being coached, they too have a model to follow when doing their ministry.

- **Ministry Doers**—By coaching people with whom they develop relationships within the context of their ministry, these doers help them to discover how God is working in their lives and to take responsibility for defining and shaping their own futures.

Anyone in your church or faith-based organization who helps others in any way will benefit greatly from learning how to coach. Whether or not they are part of an organized ministry , they are ministering to others in service to God and to the glory of Jesus Christ. Here is an example of how that happens. It comes from Tim, a graduate of our *Empowerment Coaching Training*.

I have used many of the skills taught in the coaching sessions in several areas of my life. Here are some examples.

Friends that complain about issues in life. By using the questioning techniques I learned, I have "informally" been able to help them realize what the cause of their issue really is—and if they really have one, or if they are just complaining. It has helped some stop the complaining if no real reason exists. The commitment for action and accountability techniques have helped me guide people to actually takes some steps instead of just spinning their wheels.

Home—Kids kids kids. I have used the "taking responsibility for action" very effectively. I've used the accountability process with "how will I know you've done what you said you would do?" They now know that if they say they are going to do something, they know the next two questions will be "by when?" and "how will I know you did it?" It's almost like a joke, but they are learning that they need to follow through with what they say they are going to do.

Work—Coaching techniques are very effective in dealing with vendors. Firm dates on follow up, clarification (here is what I am hearing you say) on issues/responsibility, and "peeling the onion" on excuses are just a few areas I have been able to use the coaching skills which were taught.

People who learn how to coach soon discover that their newly acquired skills impact others in ways that have often eluded them in the past. And because they no longer feel compelled to give expert advice, they find that it is possible to coach anyone in anything, anywhere, anytime. Just imagine what it would be like if a growing number of ministry coordinators, leaders, and doers in your church or organization learned and began using the power of empowerment coaching, both in their ministry relationships and in the other areas of their lives.

 ## The Coach asks . . .

- How might a ministry fall into the program trap?

- If you were to apply the *Ministry Model* to a ministry in which you are involved, how would that enable you to better achieve the purpose of serving God and glorifying Christ?

- How might you benefit from learning to coach in your ministry role?

- Who else could you impact if you stopped advising them and started coaching them?

O Read on.

WHAT DOES IT TAKE TO BECOME AN EFFECTIVE COACH?

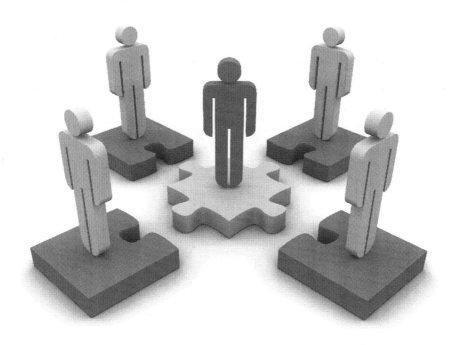

10

LEARNING *ABOUT* COACHING VERSUS LEARNING *HOW TO* COACH

If you signed up for a **sixteen-week college course on Coaching**, you would likely sit through a series of lectures on topics such as

- The Definition of Coaching
- The History of Coaching
- The Six Most Prevalent Models of Coaching
- An Integrated Model of Coaching
- The Coaching Process
- The Twelve Most Important Coaching Skills
- Measuring the Results of Coaching
- The Future of Coaching

If the material was well organized and effectively explained, and if you paid attention and took good notes, you would leave that course knowing a lot more about coaching than you had before taking it. But could you *do coaching* effectively? Not likely.

If you attended a **two-day workshop on** *How To Coach*, you probably wouldn't have to sit through lectures on topics like the history and the most prevalent models of coaching. A workshop would be more practical than that. Let's assume that your workshop instructor did the following.

- Defined coaching and explained the coaching model he or she prefers.

- Used that coaching model to explain the coaching process step by step, noting the "little things" along the way that an effective coach needs to do—and giving examples from his or her own coaching experience to illustrate those points.

- Identified and defined the twelve most important coaching skills and explained how they should be used in each step of the coaching process.

- Used various techniques to illustrate how those twelve skills should be applied to the coaching process. Those techniques included viewing video and live demonstrations of key skills and selecting a few skills for you to role play (practice), followed by discussing what you had experienced.

- Explained two ways you can measure the results of coaching.

- Handed out a list of "Coaching Tips."

If you want to learn how to coach, you would likely select the workshop over the college course. But if you did attend that workshop, could you *do coaching* effectively? Once again—not likely.

Imagine that at the end of either the course or the workshop described above you were required to coach someone for thirty minutes on a topic you knew absolutely nothing about. How confident would you be about doing that? "Not very," you're probably thinking. That's because the course and workshop described above enable you to learn *about* coaching but do not adequately equip you to leave being able to say with confidence "I am ready to coach." There's a good reason for that.

The only way to learn how to coach is by coaching. There is no short cut.

The two-day *Empowerment Coaching Training* we offer concludes with two thirty-minute practice coaching sessions. For the first session, the person being coached selects the topic, so the person coaching them has to be prepared to coach them on anything. After that, they switch roles and practice for another thirty-minute session. The reason they are prepared for those sessions is that over the past two days they have already engaged in eight practice coaching sessions. They have learned the process and coaching skills we teach by using them in real-life practice coaching situations.

Learning How to Coach

As explained in Chapter 6, to truly learn something we need to find the answers to three questions.

- What does this *mean?*
- Why is it *important?*
- How will I *use it?*

If you rely on someone else (teacher or trainer) to tell you the answers to those questions, you probably won't learn much. You need to discover those answers for yourself.

When it comes to learning how to coach, the answers you discover as you grapple with the first two questions are very important. We emphasized in Chapter 4 that the answer to the "What does coaching mean?" question is significantly influenced by sports coaching, which is the exact opposite of what we mean by coaching. The *discovery of meaning* in this case requires a change from one way of thinking to another, often referred to as a *Paradigm Shift*. We describe it as the shift from a *Telling Paradigm* to an *Empowering Paradigm*.

- *Telling Paradigm*—My role is to give you the best advice I can and persuade you to apply that advice to your own life.
- *Empowering Paradigm*—My role is to empower you to take control of and responsibility for defining and pursuing your own future.

To effectively make that paradigm shift, you must also discover your own answer to the "Why is coaching important?" question. We can tell you why we think it's important, but you won't even care about answering the "How will I use it?" question until you place your own high value on coaching.

There are many ways you can begin to discover your own answers to the *meaning* and *importance* questions. However, we have learned through our experience that the "Aha! Now I get it" light will remain rather dim until you actually experience two things.

- What it's like to be coached.
- What it's like to coach others.

That's why, since the beginning of our program, we have included ten practice coaching sessions in our sixteen-hour *Empowerment Coaching Training*. This isn't only to help people learn how to coach but also to help them both to discover what coaching is really all about and to come to their own conclusions about its value. As Jim Vidakovik points out, people retain

- 20% of what they *hear*
- 30% of what they *see*
- 50% of what they *hear* and *see*
- 70% of what they *hear, see,* and *say* (e.g., discuss, explain to others)
- 90% of what they *hear, see, say,* and *do*

(Jim Vidakovik, *Trainers in Motion: Creating a Participant-Centered Learning Environment*, AMACOM, 2000, page 25.)

Math teachers use story problems to help their students discover the meaning, importance, and application of math in lifelike situations. We use coaching practice sessions to achieve the same result.

It is our hope that by reading this book you are learning more *about* coaching. If you want to learn *how to coach,* select a training program that enables you to experience coaching and practice the coaching process and skills enough for you to be able to leave the training saying "I'm ready to coach."

Then . . . go forth and coach.

 ## The Coach asks . . .

- How would you describe the Paradigm Shift required to go from *telling* to *empowering?*

- Go back to the description of the two-day workshop on How To Coach. The fourth item down describes the various techniques used to illustrate how the twelve coaching skills should be applied to the coaching process. Why wouldn't that, along with the other items, adequately prepare you to coach? What, if anything, is missing?

- If someone were to ask you "How can I learn to coach?" What would you tell them?

◐ Read on.

11

DEVELOPING THE HEART OF A COACH

As we discussed in Chapter 10, making the shift from a *Telling Paradigm* to an *Empowering Paradigm* focuses on developing the mindset of a coach. An empowering paradigm addresses how we understand, think about, and talk about coaching. It helps us make personal judgments about the importance of coaching, and it helps to shape how we do coaching. But there's more to becoming an effective coach than having the right mindset.

One of the first questions we ask at the beginning of our training is

"What do you believe is meant by having the *heart of a coach?*"

As we listen to the different ways people try to answer this question, a common thread begins to emerge. Everyone seems to be searching their own hearts to see what they find there, and many find it difficult to articulate those findings. So we turn next to see what insights we might find in the Scriptures.

We learn in the Scriptures some valuable realities about the *heart.* As early as Genesis 6 we read *"The LORD saw how great the wickedness of the human race had become on the earth, and that every inclination of the thoughts of the human heart was only evil all the time"* (Genesis 6:5). It seems hopeless, but we know it doesn't end there. There's a way out of that "only evil all the time" trap . . .

> *"It is by grace that you have been saved, through faith—and this is not from yourselves, it is the gift of God—not by works so that no one can boast."* —Ephesians 2:9

> *"For we are God's handiwork, created in Christ Jesus to do good works, which God prepared in advance for us to do."* —Ephesians 2:10

The word "heart" is used approximately 740 times in the Bible. The references that have the most significance for us are those that represent a person's inner desires and will. Our hearts reveal our true nature and motivation. This suggests that developing the heart of a coach is even more significant than developing the mindset of a coach.

> *"I will give them a heart to know me, that I am the LORD. They will be my people, and I will be their God, for they will return to me with all their heart."* —Jeremiah 24:7

> *"'This is the covenant I will make with them after that time, says the LORD. I will put my laws in their hearts, and I will write them on their minds.'"* —Hebrews 10:16

> *"For where your treasure is, there your heart will be also."* —Luke 12:34

For coaching to be Christ centered, we need to begin by making certain that the motivations of our heart are Christ centered.

"'Teacher, which is the greatest commandment in the Law?' Jesus replied: 'Love the Lord your God with all your heart and with all your soul and with all your mind.' This is the first and greatest commandment. And the second is like it: 'Love your neighbor as yourself.' All the Law and the Prophets hang on these two commandments."—Matthew 22:36–40

Next, we need to make certain we have a clear picture of what "love your neighbor as yourself" truly means when we have an opportunity to coach that "neighbor." There are a number of passages we might use to clarify that. Our favorite is Philippians 2:1–9. As we walk our way through those verses, hopefully Paul's words will become close to your heart as well.

"If you have any encouragement from being united with Christ, if any comfort from his love, if any common sharing in the Spirit, if any tenderness and compassion, then make my joy complete by being like-minded, having the same love, being one in spirit and of one mind."—Philippians 2:1–2

By using the clause "If you have . . . ," Paul speaks directly to the true nature and motivations of our heart. It isn't simply a question of whether we understand what Christ has done for us. Paul wants to know if we experience Christ's encouragement and comfort that stem from His love for us. If they draw us close to Christ, then we have every reason for being united in spirit and mind. Are we? That's the question Paul is asking.

"Do nothing out of selfish ambition or vain conceit. Rather, in humility value others above yourselves, not looking to your own interests but each of you to the interests of the others."
—Philippians 2:3–4

Paul doesn't simply tell us to be humble. He explains exactly what that means. And he makes it clear that selfish ambition and vain conceit are more than vague concepts. How will people know that we have the true heart of a coach? When they see that we value others above ourselves and are paying special attention to their interests. That's why *listening* is such a vital coaching skill. Believe it when we say that without having the heart of a coach you will find it difficult to make the mental shift from *telling* to *empowering*.

"In your relationships with one another, have the same mindset as Christ Jesus: Who, being in very nature God, did not consider equality with God something to be used to his own advantage; rather, he made himself nothing by taking the very nature of a servant."—Philippians 2:5–7

Without a humble servant attitude, Christ could not have responded to God's calling for His human life. That becomes vividly clear when we see the extent to which his servant attitude took Him.

" . . . being made in human likeness. And being found in appearance as a man, he humbled himself by becoming obedient to death—even death on a cross!"
—Philippians 2:7–9

Effective coaching evolves from a deliberate imitation of the humble, servant posture Jesus took as our advocate. As we coach, striving to master the process and skills of coaching, we will make mistakes. But if we have the right heart, we will discover that the people we coach will still be transformed. The reverse is also true, for coaching technique without the right heart often becomes manipulation.

We serve by coaching, and we coach by serving—serving that comes from the heart.

 ## The Coach asks . . .

- How would you now answer the question "What do you believe is meant by having *the heart of a coach*?"

- When people give advice, mentor, counsel, or teach, we often feel as though they are talking down to us—even when they have a genuine desire to help us. How does coaching enable us to come across in a way that is more consistent with what Paul advocates in Philippians 2:1–9?

◗ Read on.

12

BECOMING EQUIPPED TO COACH ANYONE ON ANYTHING

Early in our *Empowerment Coaching Training* program, we ask participants to set a goal for the training by filling in the blanks to complete this statement . . .

My goal is to be able to coach _____ in _____.

That brief exercise suggests that they will probably want to focus their coaching by identifying specifically WHO they want to coach, as well as WHAT will be their area of specialization. We ask that question knowing that they may be apprehensive about coaching in areas where they feel they cannot give "expert" advice. Drawing on what we discussed in Chapter 4, that is due in large part to the influence of the sports coaching model. After all, what college or professional level football coach have you seen cross over to become a basketball coach? But remember also what Sir John Whitmore said about the lesson learned from Tim Gallwey's book,

The Inner Game of Tennis: "Gallwey was the first to demonstrate a simple and comprehensive method of coaching that could be readily applied to almost any situation" (J. Whitmore, *Coaching for Performance*, 1992, p. 7).

As we continue through the explanation and discussion of *Empowerment Coaching*, the "method of coaching that could be readily applied to almost any situation" begins to take root. At the end of that discussion, we ask, "What can you do if the person you are coaching elects to focus on an area you know nothing about?" After talking about that a bit, we ask them to revisit the goal they set for the training—and challenge them to change that goal to

My goal is to be able to coach *anyone* in *anything, anytime, anywhere.*

In the coaching profession, you will find coaches specializing in specific areas. The categories most frequently found are

- *Life Coaching*—Focused on individuals who wish to make some form of significant change to gain greater fulfillment and balance in their life.
- *Business Coaching*—Directed toward individuals wanting to achieve business-related goals. This includes self-employed professionals and small business owners.
- *Executive Coaching*—Provided to top executives and senior managers whose performance impacts the whole organization and who often find that "it's lonely at the top."
- *Career Coaching*—Directed toward helping people find new employment or change their career direction. Increasingly today this is the focus of outplacement services.

Beyond these broad categories, you will often find professional coaches identifying their focus in more specific terms: Christian

Coach, Entrepreneurial Coach, Writing Coach, Teen Coach, Performance Coach, Personal Development Coach, Leadership Coach, Sales Coach, Confidence Coach, Public Speaking Coach, Diversity Coach, Parenting Coach, Success Coach, Life Improvement Coach, Financial Coach, . . . and the list goes on.

If they are trained to "coach anyone in anything," why don't professional coaches simply call themselves a *coach* and work with anyone who comes their way? There are essentially two reasons.

1. Coaching is one of the fastest growing human-development professions in the world. At this point, however, there are no state licensing requirements. That means that the cost of entry is low. It also means that people are calling themselves a "coach" without having been trained, and too often without really understanding how coaching differs from giving expert advice. Using a very specialized label may mean that their approach will be to "tell you what to do and how to do it." It's important to find out what their understanding of and approach to coaching includes.

2. Coaches who are well trained and skilled will often select a specialized label for marketing purposes. In other words, the label they have selected defines the niche market they are trying to reach. Their background, education, and expertise will be recognized primarily by people seeking that particular specialized help.

Coaching Anyone on Anything

There are advantages to coaching someone in an area in which you yourself have experience and expertise. You will be able to identify more closely with what this individual is experiencing.

After they have identified options for a decision they have to make, you might be able to suggest another option for them to consider—which you would do only if they welcomed that suggestion.

But as you might expect at this point, there are also disadvantages. You might start asking leading questions to gently "push" them in the direction you believe they should go. Or you could easily slip into giving "expert" advice.

The fact is that the more opportunities you have to coach anyone on anything, the better your coaching skills and technique will become. There are two coaching concepts that describe the types of skills you need to develop.

- **Being There**—Allow the person you are coaching to define the direction and set the pace of the coaching conversation. This requires being open to wherever they are at the moment, and it may include stopping at times and allowing them to express how they are feeling about something that is "right now" in their life.

- **Coaching Moment by Moment**—Never try to anticipate what the person will say next, and never allowing yourself to "tune out" and start thinking about what you will say or ask next. This discipline requires that you listen intently to what the person is saying and wait until they are finished before determining your next question or comment.

You will typically initiate a coaching conversation by asking "What would you like to talk about?" That leaves the direction of the conversation totally open to whatever is on their mind. They may respond with exactly what you expected, or they may introduce something that is totally unexpected. Regardless of what they say, you need to be there, coaching moment by moment.

There are several factors related to coaching that make that possible.

- People come to you for help because in some area of their life they are thinking "Where I am now is not where I want to be, and I could use some help closing that gap."

- Their answer to your "What would you like to talk about?" question defines the coaching focus. As you listen and continue asking probing questions, they will reach a point where they begin telling you about that gap.

- At the appropriate point, you will typically ask, "What specifically would you like to accomplish?" You will then help them turn their answer into a goal statement.

- Regardless of what they want to achieve, they are the expert in that area. Whatever it is they need to learn, they will take responsibility for that learning. You will not offer to teach them.

- In everything you do, you will be empowering them to take control of and responsibility for defining and pursuing their own future.

As you continue with them, your coaching efforts will focus on

- Asking them to set action steps to be completed by a set date before your next coaching conversation.

- Helping them to overcome any obstacles standing in their way and to avoid distractions that might pull them off track.

- Encouraging them and celebrating achievements with them as they complete their action steps and move toward achieving their goal.

That, briefly, is the coaching process. The only expertise you need is the development of the heart and mind of a coach and mastery of the skills of empowerment coaching. Then you will be able to coach anyone in anything, anytime, anywhere.

If that is your goal, and we can help you in any way, please contact us. Professional coaches/trainers are prepared to bring this valuable training to your doorstep. Or you can visit us in beautiful West Michigan for one of our two-day public training workshops. The training schedule is on our website:

Website: http://www.empowermentcoachingnetwork.com/church/ectraining.html

Mike McGervey & Tim Cosby

ABOUT THE AUTHORS

Mike McGervey

Mike provides professional development coaching for small business owners, home businesses, self-employed professionals, and church leaders. Mike is the author of the *Empowerment Coaching Training* program.

Email: mike@empowermentcoachingnetwork.com

Tim Cosby

Tim provides personal development coaching to Christian leaders and team-building seminars for churches and Christian organizations. He previously served on the pastoral team of Bella Vista Church in Rockford, MI, and was Dean of Spiritual Formation at Cornerstone University.

Email: timlifecoach@gmai.com

Mike and Tim are cofounders of the Empowerment Coaching Network www.empowermentcoachingnetwork.com

WHAT EMPOWERMENT COACHING TRAINING GRADUATES ARE SAYING . . .

This was a very hands-on conference that actually allowed us to immediately put into practice what we were being taught. The role plays were an excellent way to give us a chance to deal with real-life situations. By actually coaching and being coached, I was able to see how valuable this service is. Thank you for providing a nonthreatening place to learn more! —L.N.

This is outstanding training. I have been to other coaching training, and this is much more thorough and comprehensive. It gave me a solid basis for coaching that can be used in other contexts as well. Thank you! —R.B.

The two days of coach training proved to be intense, exhausting, and some of the most rewarding work I've ever been engaged in. When you're sitting face to face with a partner, coaching and being coached, things happen to you that you couldn't have anticipated. The facilitators walked us through challenging territory. —K.B.

This two-day workshop was a very effective way for me to learn the skills and grasp the significance of the very powerful tool of coaching. Focusing on the discovery process with the person being coached empowers them to set in motion a plan of action for accomplishing their goals and equips them to be and dowhat God wants for them. Coaching is a transformational tool in God's Kingdom. —A.H.

Empowerment Coaching Training gave me the tools necessary to define reality, set the desired goal, and then line up specific steps that would lead towards the goal. I leave the seminar knowing how to coach anyone in anything, anywhere, and at any time. This is a huge accomplishment, and I thank God for the ECT training. —D.B.

Empowerment Coaching Training benefited me greatly in that it gave me the language and skills needed to help peers formulate action plans for their personal agendas. Interaction with class members was an additional bonus, making the training session enjoyable. —F.S.

Empowerment Coaching Training was filled with practical material, well presented. It gave me a new confidence in coaching. The hands-on approach was helpful. The focus on transformative empowerment rather than imparting information is excellent. It takes the fear out of coaching and provides a tool that can be used in any conversation or relationship. —S.A.

The process presented in the coaching training gave me an excellent foundation upon which to build a practical ministry to pastors. —D.S

MPOWERMENT COACHING TRAINING

mpowerment Coaching raining — a 16-hour ccelerated learning xperience that will help you levelop the heart, mind, and kills of an effective coach.

raining highlights . . .

- Assessing your *Coaching Readiness*.
- Helping those you coach define their *Coaching Focus*.
- Mastering the 7 Key Elements of the *Coaching Conversation*.
- Learning to coach *Moment-by-Moment*.
- Enabling those you coach to stay on their *Critical Path*.

'ou learn to coach best by coaching. During the 16-hour training, you will iave an opportunity to apply what 'ou are learning in 10 coaching iractice sessions. Each participant eceives a 62-page workbook and esource manual.

FREE Introductory Presentation for Your Church or Organization

Our 30- to 45-minute presentation for your church or organization that explains the benefits of coaching by focusing on 3 questions addressed in this book . . .

- ▶ *Why coaching?*
- ▶ *What is it like to be coached?*
- ▶ *What does it take to become an effective coach?*

The Coaching Based Leader
eNewsletter — **FREE** subscription
www.coachingbasedministry.com

Empowerment CoachingNetwork

How to Empower People to become the Architects of their Future.

Made in the USA
Lexington, KY
30 April 2018